My Sandwich

Words and Music by Lillian Anderson

Illustrated by Elizabeth Uhlig

Marble House Editions

Published by Marble House Editions
96-09 66th Avenue (Suite 1D)
Rego Park, NY 11374
elizabeth.uhlig@yahoo.com
www.marble-house-editions.com

Library of Congress Cataloguing-in-Publication Data
Anderson, Lillian
My Sandwich/by Lillian Anderson

Summary: An illustrated rhyming poem and song for young readers.

ISBN 978-0-9834030-3-6
Library of Congress Catalog Card Number 2011944477

Production date: March, 2012
Plant & location: Printed by Everbest Printing (Guangzhou, China), Co. Ltd
Job / Batch# 106079

Printed in China

For my son, Joseph,

the inventor and consumer of all my sandwiches!

I made myself a **sandwich**
that was
six inches thick.

And when I ate
my sandwich
it almost made me sick.

First I put
bologna,
Did you **listen**
to what I said?

Next I added **pickles**
on top of a
slice of bread.

Pickles, bologna, on top of a **slice of bread.**

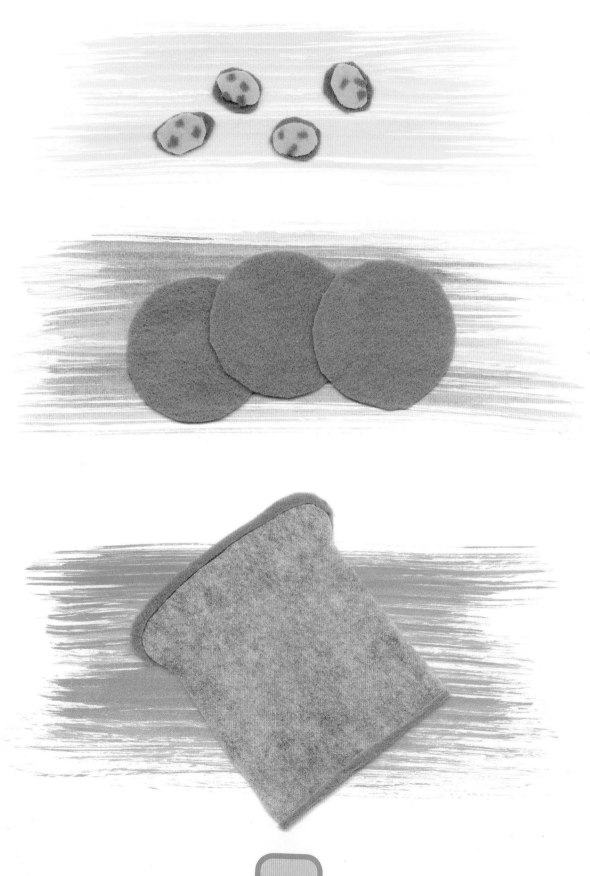

Then I put
salami,
Did you **listen**
to what I said?

Next I added **olives,**
on top of a
slice of bread.

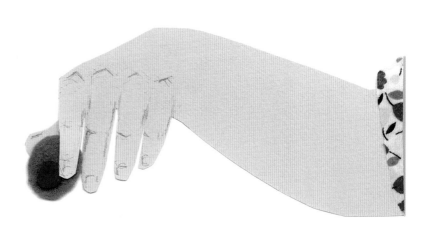

Olives,
salami,
pickles,
bologna,
on top of a
slice of bread.

Then I put the **roast beef,**
Did you **listen**
to what I said?

Next I added
mustard,
on top of a
slice of bread.

Mustard,
roast beef,
olives,
salami,
pickles,
bologna,
on top of a
slice of bread.

Then I put some
ham and **cheese,**
Did you
listen
to what I said?

Next I added
mayonnaise,
on top of a
slice of bread.

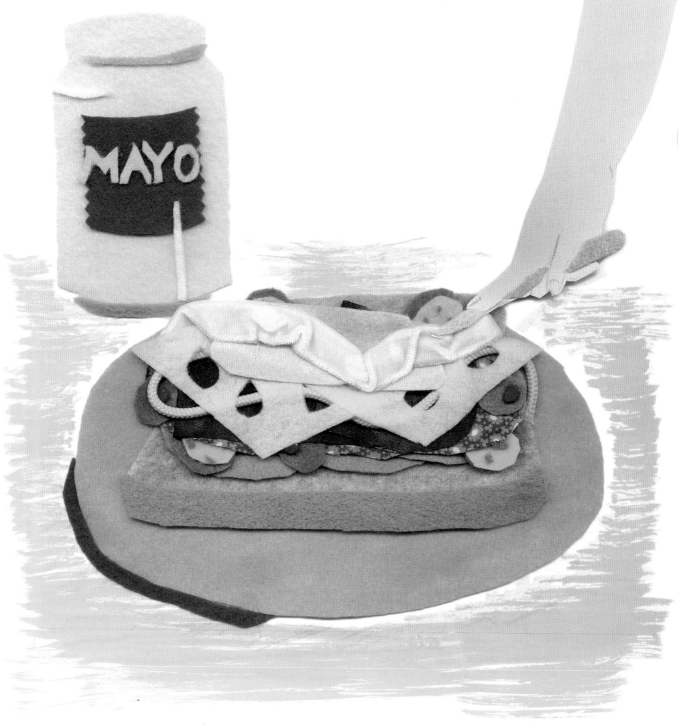

Mayonnaise, some **ham** and **cheese, mustard,**

roast beef, olives, salami,

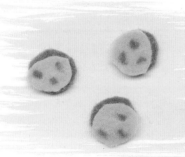 

pickles, **bologna,**

on top of a **slice of bread**.

Then I put
tomatoes.
Did you **listen**
to what I said?

Last I added **lettuce,**

...and a
second
slice of **bread.**

Lettuce,
tomatoes,

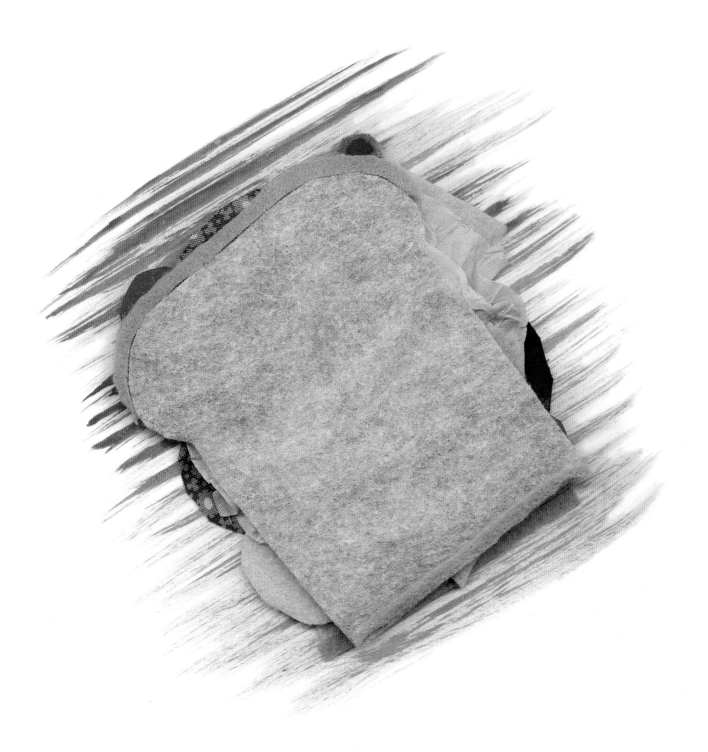

ham and cheese,
mayonnaise,

mustard,
roast beef,

olives,
salami,

pickles,
bologna,

on top of a
slice of bread.

And then I went to bed!

My Sandwich
Words and music by Lillian Anderson © 2001

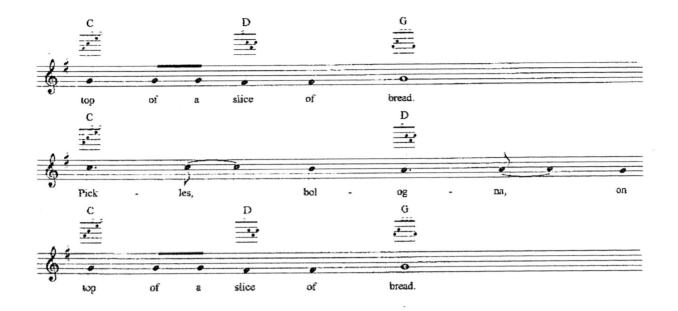

1. Then I put salami, did you listen to what I said?
   Next I added olives on top of a slice of bread.
   Olives, salami, pickles, bologna on top of a slice of bread.

2. Then I put the roast beef, did you listen to what I said?
   Next I added mustard on top of a slice of bread.
   Mustard, roast beef, olives, salami, pickles, bologna on top of a slice of bread.

3. Then I put some ham and cheese, did you listen to what I said?
   Next I added mayonnaise on top of a slice of bread.
   Mayonnaise, ham and cheese, mustard, roast beef, olives, salami,
      pickles, bologna on top of a slice of bread.

4. Then I put tomatoes, did you listen to what I said?
   Last I added lettuce and a second slice of bread.
   Lettuce, tomatoes, mayonnaise, ham and cheese, mustard, roast beef,
      olives, salami, pickles, bologna on top of a slice of bread.

   And then I went to bed!

About the Author

Lillian Anderson is a composer and musician who has also been a music teacher for young children. While teaching, Ms. Anderson wrote songs for her students and has recorded a children's CD of original songs and folktales.

To learn more about Ms. Anderson and her work, or to purchase her CD's, please refer to www.cdbaby.com/cd/lillian.

Ms. Anderson may also be reached at lillianderson@hotmail.com.